"Tara Beth writes from a deep belief that the ancient [...] power today as when John first penned them. With [...] her readers to experience the light of Jesus through [...] study series, integrating video, personal reflection, group discussion, and prayer. The engaged reader will find new freedom."
Mandy Smith, pastor and author of *The Vulnerable Pastor*

"In a world full of chaos, confusion, and contention, we desperately need to accept 'An Invitation to Light.' Tara Beth leads us into a deep dive of the letters of John, where we discover how to be light and hope in the midst of darkness and despair."
Christine Caine, founder of A21 and Propel Women

"This Bible study experience is rich with love and wisdom. It will serve as a valuable resource for any small group or personal study. Tara Beth Leach gently, intentionally, and powerfully invites us to dig deeper into God's words. She challenges us into greater hope—something we all need in this day and age."
Faith Eury Cho, pastor, speaker, and author of *Experiencing Friendship with God*

"I highly recommend this six-week experience crafted for groups and individuals by Tara Beth Leach. With her skills as a teacher of the Word, Tara Beth provides the context for understanding the teachings of the apostle John. Then the author stirs our thinking with probing group exercises and questions, moments of reflection, and beautifully crafted prayers. Engaging in this experience has the potential to move the reader from accumulating information to being formed as a child of the light."
Nancy Beach, leadership coach and author of *Next Sunday: An Honest Dialogue About the Future of the Church*

"Tara Beth Leach's *Live in the Light* is the work of a master teacher. A deeply reflective, emotionally engaging, scholarly but accessible guide into the depths of the epistles of John. Join with your friends and take this six-week journey. Grow into the light of the one who reigns over the whole world."
David Fitch, Lindner Chair of Evangelical Theology at Northern Seminary

"When it seems bad news is daily scrolling across our screens, our souls are scouring for good news. Look no further than the book of John. *Live in the Light* brings to the surface the radiance of Jesus—the Good News. Tara Beth Leach knows Jesus and it's from that close relationship that she guides us into courageous and surprising discoveries of who Jesus can be to us now. This six-week study is much more than a search for knowledge—it's an interactive experience!"
Dan White Jr., cofounder of the KINEO Center and author of *Love Over Fear*

"Tara Beth Leach trains our eyes to recognize the radiance of the life being offered to us. For John, light is the way of speaking of truth amid a world of falsehood and false teachers; it's a way of inviting us from secrecy to confession; it's a way of calling us from an old order to God's new creation. As a pastor, Tara Beth recognizes John's pastoral urgency, and she translates it for our world today. This beautiful study will help you slow down and see the light—more than that, it will help you live fully alive within it."

Glenn Packiam, lead pastor of Rockharbor Church in Costa Mesa, California, and author of *The Resilient Pastor*

"John is close to my heart, and we don't read his letters enough. Tara Beth Leach is a faithful guide to this important part of Scripture, inviting it to change our hearts, minds, and lives."

Beth Felker Jones, professor of theology at Northern Seminary

"With her trademark wisdom, warmth, and pastoral precision, Tara Beth Leach guides us toward illumination and insight that cuts through the fog of despair and darkness so many of us feel today. *Live in the Light* is a spectacular companion for a deep dive into the Gospel of John."

Jay Kim, pastor and author of *Analog Christian*

"There are few people I trust more to guide me through the Word of God than Tara Beth Leach. With a strong heart, pastoral sensitivity, and a soul immersed in the light of the Spirit and hope of Jesus, Tara Beth gives us fresh eyes to see Jesus and experience the gifts of the Spirit through the letters of John. She is a trusted counselor, visionary leader, and deep lover of Jesus."

Sean Palmer, speaker, coach, and author of *Speaking by the Numbers*

TARA BETH LEACH

LIVE IN THE LIGHT

Radiating the Hope
of the Letters of John

An imprint of InterVarsity Press
Downers Grove, Illinois

InterVarsity Press
P.O. Box 1400 | Downers Grove, IL 60515-1426
ivpress.com | email@ivpress.com

InterVarsity Press® is the publishing division of InterVarsity Christian Fellowship/USA®. For more information, visit intervarsity.org.

Cover design: David Fassett
Interior design: Jeanna Wiggins
Images: © Eglelip / iStock / Getty Images Plus via Getty Images

ISBN 978-1-5140-0682-5 (print) | ISBN 978-1-5140-0683-2 (digital)

Printed in the United States of America ♾

Library of Congress Cataloging-in-Publication Data
Names: Leach, Tara Beth, 1982- author.
Title: Live in the light : radiating the hope of the letters of John-a
  six-week Bible study experience / Tara Beth Leach.
Description: Downers Grove, IL : InterVarsity Press, 2024. | Series: IVP
  Bible studies
Identifiers: LCCN 2024004999 (print) | LCCN 2024005000 (ebook) | ISBN
  9781514006825 (print) | ISBN 9781514006832 (digital)
Subjects: LCSH: Bible. Epistles of John. | Christian life--Biblical
  teaching. | BISAC: RELIGION / Biblical Studies / Bible Study Guides |
  RELIGION / Christian Living / Spiritual Growth
Classification: LCC BS2805.6.C48 L43 2024 (print) | LCC BS2805.6.C48
  (ebook) | DDC 227/.9406--dc23/eng/20240224
LC record available at https://lccn.loc.gov/2024004999
LC ebook record available at https://lccn.loc.gov/2024005000

30   29   28   27   26   25   24 | 8   7   6   5   4   3   2   1

CONTENTS

Creation groans for more.
She aches as the world spins with war.
She waits in hopes for healing.

As the wind roars, rages, and whips,
Sacred invitations erupt from the
      Savior's lips.
"Come, my children, come one,
      come all, come kneeling."

AN INVITATION TO LIGHT

Not too long ago, I was driving my boys to school on the most beautiful fall day. Leaves were starting to turn, I had a pumpkin-flavored coffee in my hand, I had just finished a fulfilling workout, and my boys were happily chatting in the backseat. I had nothing but joy in my heart and my mind, and I found myself thanking God for the gift of my children and the gift of the day. I hugged and kissed my boys goodbye and watched them saunter into the school as they chatted with their friends, when suddenly, fear darkened my heart.

What if . . .

Another horrific mass shooting had happened and the thought of such a scene dampened my joy.

It's the *What if?* questions that lurk around the corners of every joyful day. What-if situations exist for all of us, and they can be downright frightening. On that day, for me, it was a school shooting. Your what-if fear could be job loss, illness, or loneliness. Sometimes, darkness seems to overcome, drown, and penetrate. Click on the news, and despair comes knocking on the doors of our emotions. Even as Christians, we wonder, *What do we do? What is God going to do? Is there any hope? Will the light eventually win?*

At the heart of Scripture is a robust call for the people of God to bear witness to the light of God amid a weary, groaning, and dark world. To be a witness means we are called to be ambassadors of the kingdom of God. To be a witness means we are called to mirror the things of God—

the goodness of God, the light of God, and the love of God. *Bearing witness* means that we are to resemble the characteristics of God, so that when people look at us they will see what God is like. At the heart of the letters of John in the New Testament is a vision for such a witness—that is, to live light and hope when darkness seems to be looming. In the end, light wins. In the present, light is here. In the now, we are called to live the light.

The apostle John, the author of these three letters—who also authored the fourth Gospel earlier in his life and the book of Revelation later in his life—is referred to as "the beloved disciple" of Jesus. John followed in the footsteps of his rabbi, Jesus. He witnessed Jesus turning water into wine; he stood by as Jesus healed the invalid near the waters of Bethesda; he witnessed the wonder of Jesus feeding five thousand with only a few loaves and fishes; he was there at the transfiguration; he followed Jesus to the cross and cared for Jesus' mother, Mary; and he was one of the first to hear the news of the empty tomb. In the book of Acts, we see that John became one of the first leaders of the early Christian church.

Some years later, John wrote letters to turbulent churches rife with leadership failures, divisions over theology and practice, church splits, and even an infamous "antichrist" who convinced faithful Christians to revolt.

Maybe that sounds eerily similar. It does to me. It seems as though the church is melting under the heat wave of national politics and conspiracy theories, divisions over race and justice, wars raging in the backyards of innocent civilians (sometimes in the name of Christianity!), and hunger raging in the bellies of infants. Where do we stand as a church? Does the world see the light and hope in *us* amid the darkness?

As a pastor, I feel the weightiness of John's letters. He writes as one who knows division, church splits, struggle, and ongoing conflict. At the same time, John writes because he believes in Jesus and he believes in the church. John believed the words of Jesus when he said, "I have told you these things, so that in me you may have peace. In this world you will have trouble. But take heart! I have overcome the world" (John 16:33). We do have trouble in our world today, but Jesus has indeed overcome the world.

For John, the future of the church is not a lost cause. He does not believe his words will be in vain, but instead he recognizes the authority given to him as an apostle, a pastor, a church planter, and an elder. He gives a vision for radiance—that is, as the light of Jesus fills our lives, it exudes and beams out of us and cuts through the darkness. It's the kind of radiance that flows out of our relationship with God and one another—one that is wrapped in light, in which God is the source of all these things.

When I think of things such as these, I can't help but imagine what could happen if Jesus' people took John's clarion call to heart. To live a radiant Christian life is to reflect and emit the truth, light, love, and freedom of Jesus—it is to *glow in darkness.* Thus, the invitation John gives to the reader is an invitation to a life of beaming light.

Over the next six weeks, listen for John's invitations to the earliest Christians and the invitations for us today. The backdrop of the world in which we live is full of bitterness, war, strife, abuse, and misery. We are surrounded by the despairing, hurting, and hopeless. The world needs Jesus, and the world needs to know that Jesus' family is like Jesus. When the church is truly light, others are drawn into the love and truth of Jesus through our fellowship.

This is a six-week study with weekly teachings and group discussions and five days of individual study per week. It walks through the letters of John and also includes other books of the Bible, especially written by John the apostle. It is recommended that group time be a minimum of sixty to ninety minutes so that groups can have plenty of time for prayer requests and fellowship as well as the video teaching and group discussion. Plan to pick five days a week for individual study that should take about fifteen to twenty minutes per day. Days one through four include readings and written reflections, and day five is a guided prayer practice.

My prayer for you is that over the next six weeks, the light of Jesus and his truth would bathe you in his love, light, and forgiveness. I don't know where you find yourself these days; whether you're new in your Christian journey or a mature Christian, I pray that this study would grow you. May the Lord meet with you in every moment, and may Jesus embolden you to truth; may the Spirit empower you to freedom; may the Lord propel you to love; and may the Father impel you to light.

HOW TO USE
THIS BOOK

Whether you are engaging in this study with a large group, a small group, in a coffee shop with a friend, or by yourself in your favorite chair, here are some helpful suggestions.

For the Group Session . . .

Set aside a designated day and time for a weekly gathering—in person or virtually—for the next six weeks. The content (video and discussion) will take about an hour, but I recommend allowing some additional time for a check-in or to share prayer requests.

The videos are accessed through the QR code in the book. These videos were created with a group in mind—that you would watch the video together and then immediately engage in the content that follows. But it means that individuals also have access, which is nice if someone has to miss a group gathering.

A few tips on engaging in a group discussion:

- Be willing to participate in the discussion. The leader of your group will moderate the conversation, and it helps them to have willing participants.
- Be careful not to dominate the discussion. We are sometimes so eager to express our thoughts that we leave too little opportunity for others to respond. By all means participate, but also make space for others' contributions.
- Be sensitive to the other members of the group. Listen attentively— you might be surprised by their insights!

- When possible, link what you say to the comments of others. This will encourage some of the more hesitant members of the group to participate.

- Stick to the topic being discussed and try to avoid "rabbit trails."

- Expect God to teach you through the content being discussed and through the other members of the group.

- Pray that you will have an enjoyable and profitable time together, but also that as a result of the study you will find ways to respond individually or even as a group.

- Remember that anything said in the group is considered confidential and should not be discussed outside the group unless specific permission is given to do so.

If you have time, a good check-in question might be to name a highlight from the previous week of study—either from the group session or individual days. This study is designed so that you can still participate in the group session even if you haven't done all the homework, but—of course—I think you'll still *want* to engage with everything!

For the Individual Days . . .

Following the group session are five days of content for you to engage with during the week between group gatherings. I wrote this study with you in mind—so the content is meaningful but not overwhelming, and it's designed to fit into your normal, everyday life.

A few tips for engaging in individual study and reflection:

- As you begin each day, invite God to speak to you through his Word.

- Write your answers to the questions in the spaces provided or in a journal. Writing can bring clarity and deeper understanding.

- Keep your Bible handy—you'll be using it to look up passages. Sometimes I find it's helpful to look up a passage in another translation, and most often I use an app on my phone for that.

- It might also be helpful to have a Bible dictionary handy to look up any unfamiliar words, names, or places.

- A the end of each day, thank God for what you have learned and pray about any applications that have come to mind.

AN INVITATION TO KNOW THE RADIANT ONE

GROUP SESSION INTRODUCTION

Begin group sessions with conversation, prayer, and an opener question. Following this, watch the video together followed by the group discussion.

This week we will unpack 1 John 1:1-4 and supporting passages. The ultimate invitation throughout this study is to accept the call to live a radiant Christian life. But first, we must get to know Jesus, the radiant King.

- Take a few minutes to share introductions if your group isn't already acquainted.
- Discuss the following question: What is the best invitation you've ever received in the mail?
- Read 1 John 1 aloud. As you listen, remember that this is exactly how it would have been received for the recipients of the letter. There would be a reader and the church would sit and listen. As you hear the words, ask the Lord that you would have an open heart and mind to receive these transformative words.

VIDEO
WATCH the opening video.

GROUP DISCUSSION

In the video, I describe a vacation experience that wasn't the same without my husband. More than anything, I wanted to experience it with *him*.

1. Recall and describe a time that you have experienced something so profound that you wanted others to experience it with you.

Have you ever thought about the incarnation of Jesus—that is, Jesus as fully God and also fully human? John echoes his own words found in the beginning of John 1:1-5 and points to the divine and human reality of the incarnation. Jesus is Lord and Jesus is flesh. This is an important theme in the letters of John, as there were those within the church who did not believe in the humanity of Jesus. John pastorally longs to see the churches unified over this important truth. Jesus is divine and Jesus is human. Not only that, but John has seen, heard, and felt this to be true.

2. Read 1 John 1:3-4 aloud. Notice that John talks about two different expressions of fellowship. What are these different expressions?

3. The invitation to share in fellowship is both vertical and horizontal. What is the outcome of this fellowship (see v. 4)?

Constantine Campbell writes in *1, 2, and 3 John* (The Story of God Bible Commentary):

> Perhaps we need to meditate afresh on what exactly Jesus means to us and what he could mean to others. Perhaps we need the refreshment that God's Spirit can provide so that we are not only filled with joy in our fellowship with Christ, but we are also filled with joy at the prospect of making him known. Above all, let us cherish the precious fellowship we have with God in Christ and allow its benefits to overflow to many.

As Campbell beautifully highlights, precious fellowship with Jesus creates what I call "an overflow effect." When we get to know Jesus, the Radiant One, and we discover the joy of fellowship with him, radiance and joy overflows from our lives and to the world around us.

4. Who do you know that embodies the joy of the Lord?

■ What characteristics are unique about that person?

■ In what ways did that individual's joy impact your life and the lives of others around you?

John had firsthand knowledge of the kind of joy that is born out of fellowship with Jesus and fellowship with one another. The Greek word for fellowship is *koinōnia*, which means to share things in common—to share things such as purpose, community, belongings, and labor. This kind of fellowship is with God's people and with the Trinity. The result of *koinōnia* is joy.

In John's Gospel, we see Jesus' call to this kind of intimate fellowship in John 15. Jesus proclaims that when we fellowship (abide) with him, the outflow is joy. Jesus says, "As the Father has loved me, so have I loved you. Now remain in my love. If you keep my commands, you will remain in my love, just as I have kept my father's commands and remain in his love. I have told you this so that my joy may be in you and that your joy may be complete" (John 15:9-11).

John's invitation is to personally know or have firsthand knowledge of knowing Jesus, so that we would have a growing relationship with God that produces joy (John 15:11). John writes all of this because he knows this to be personally true.

Take a few moments to discuss what you know to be true about Jesus.

5. How has knowing Jesus shaped your life?

*If the idea of "having firsthand knowledge" of Jesus or even "knowing Jesus" is a new concept for you, consider talking to your group leader or a pastor within your church.

6. Considering these truths about Jesus, does the community around you know these to be true through the life of your local church? How so or why not?

Reflecting the truths of Jesus to our neighbors begins with *fellowship* with Jesus. Much like John experienced firsthand, when we discover for ourselves the truths of Jesus, radiance is a natural outflow of those who abide. That invitation is before you today—to ask, to say, to converse, to fellowship, and to *know*. Will you accept the invitation? The invitation for the next six weeks is to give of yourself to the presence of God each day in reflection, study, and prayer. If you don't already have a daily established time for reflection, decide now when you will carve out that time.

7. Share what you plan to do for your daily time of reflection. If you already have a rhythm, share about that with the group.

8. Take a few moments to share prayer requests as you wrap up.

CLOSING PRAYER

Jesus, we thank you that you not only invite us to your table,
but you take us by the hand and walk with us to radiance.
To the weary, you say, "Come, my grace is sufficient."
To the hungry, you say, "Come, feast at my table."
To the hurting, you say, "Come and receive my comfort."
To the despairing, you say, "Come, at my table is hope."
To the broken, you say, "Come and be healed."
To the doubtful, you say, "Come, your doubts are welcome here."
To the lonely, you say, "Come to the fellowship at the table."
To that, Lord, we say yes. Amen.

Day One

BEGIN WITH THE WORD

Read 1 John 1:1-4

1. After reading it once, take a few moments to list the words or phrases that describe something about the nature of Jesus.

2. Read John 1:1-5. After reading it once, take a few moments to list the words or phrases that describe something about the nature of Jesus.

Notice the similarities? The writer of John's Gospel is—yes, you guessed it—the same writer as the letters of John. The letters were written between c. AD 86 and 88 and were believed to have been written after the Gospel. It is almost immediately noticeable that John is drawing from similar imagery as his Gospel.

John was the fisherman who followed Jesus in the inner circle of twelve other disciples who eventually became apostles. This means John spent time with Jesus and is writing about what he saw, touched, learned, and heard. He writes to draw the readers back to the one and true King, Jesus.

In both the Gospel and this letter, John refers to Jesus as "the Word," or in the original language, *logos.* This word *logos* carried weight to the readers of the early church. In the book of Genesis, God created the earth, the heavens, and all that has breath through spoken word, or *logos.* In the ancient Greek world, *logos* was a philosophical term that came to mean the force that brought life and meaning to the universe.

John reclaims this word in vivid ways for the earliest readers. The *logos* is King Jesus, the incarnate one—fully human and fully divine. *Logos* is the revelation of God in the Old Testament and the force behind and within all of creation and all that has life. *Logos* is King Jesus, the force, center, ruler, and living embodiment of God's creative power; he was there at the beginning and is actively working even today to create and redeem his creation. *Logos* is the Radiant One.

John not only penned the letters of John and the Gospel of John, but he also is the writer of the book of Revelation. Drawing from powerful and apocalyptic imagery, John envisages seeing Jesus in the glory of the new heaven and new earth. Just as John invited us to discover the fellowship of Jesus in his first few sentences of 1 John, he now draws us to the divinity of Jesus.

3. Read Revelation 19:6-13, and as you read it, underline any descriptions you see about Jesus.

The Jesus we read about is the very same Jesus that John has "heard, seen, and touched." This is the same Jesus in which he "proclaims" and writes to make his "joy complete." This Jesus—the *logos*—is who he says he is. He is the creative force behind all that is good and beautiful. He is the revelation of God—God who is love.

4. Finish the following sentences. (This isn't a quiz, just an exercise. Write what comes to mind. Let your sentences be an act of worship and praise to Jesus!)

■ Jesus was present in the beginning, and I can know that because . . .

◼ Jesus is present today and I've seen him working when . . .

◼ I thank you, Jesus, for . . .

5. You, reader, are invited to know Jesus in his humanity and his divinity—to know, to marvel, and to worship the revelation of God in Christ. In closing, write a prayer of praise and wonder to King Jesus, the Radiant One.

Day Two

BEGIN WITH THE WORD

Read 1 John 1:3-4

John testifies that he has seen Jesus. In other words, Jesus was more than a doctrine or mere idea. Jesus was a known and experienced reality. Even after his death and resurrection, Jesus *continued* to be an experienced reality, not just personally, but corporately.

1. Reread verses 3-4. What are the pronouns John uses when describing the experienced reality of Jesus?

As we reviewed two days ago, the Greek word John uses for fellowship is *koinōnia,* which means to share things in common. There was great joy in coming together and experiencing the presence of Jesus.

2. What happens when our faith is privatized?

3. Why is it so important for the Christian life to be lived together in community?

Christian community is about experiencing Jesus *together*. As I often tell the people I pastor, "I need you; you need me; we need you; you need us." In other words, there are days I need to draw on the faith and prayers of others to get through the day. And there are days I need to hear the church sing the songs I don't have the strength to sing. There are times when my gifts and talents propel others in their faith. Not only that, but when we come together, Jesus is surely there and our light shines brighter.

4. In closing, write a prayer for those in your small group. Thank God for them and their gifts, and pray that you would be able to encourage them in their walk with Jesus.

Day Three

BEGIN WITH THE WORD

Read 1 John 1:5-7

Most scholars agree that the message here is a continuation of John's declaration of Jesus: God is the source of light, and the light is witnessed in the very life of Jesus. Jesus himself said, "Anyone who has seen me has seen the Father" (John 14:9).

The relationship between God and light is woven throughout the entire tapestry of Scripture.

1. Read the following passages:

    ■ And God said, "Let there be light," and there was light. (Genesis 1:3)

    ■ For with you is the fountain of life; in your light we see light. (Psalm 36:9)

    ■ Send me your light and your faithful care, let them lead me; let them bring me to your holy mountain, to the place where you dwell. (Psalm 43:3)

    ■ The LORD wraps himself in light as with a garment; he stretches out the heavens like a tent. (Psalm 104:2)

    ■ His splendor was like the sunrise; rays flashed from his hand, where his power was hidden. (Habakuk 3:4)

    ■ The sun will no more be your light by day, nor will the brightness of the moon shine on you, for the LORD will be your everlasting light, and your God will be your glory. Your sun will never set again, and your moon will wane no more; the LORD will be your everlasting light, and your days of sorrow will end. (Isaiah 60:19-20)

- When Jesus spoke again to the people, he said, "I am the light of the world. Whoever follows me will never walk in darkness, but will have the light of life." (John 8:12)

2. What did you notice about the connection between light and God?

Take a few moments to reflect on the power of light. Without light in our world, life would not exist as we know it today. Light permeates our everyday reality and floods our days. Whether it's a twinkle, a flame, electricity, a spark, a star, or a burning ball in the sky, light strings all of life together. Light bursts in the morning and illuminates the textures, ridges, mountain tops, and glistening water in the ocean. Light fills every corner of God's very good creation. Consider the infiltrating *power* of light. This kind of infiltrating power is an image of our triune God. Jesus is our beacon, our source, our power, our guide; Jesus is the Radiant One. Jesus asks from us a surrendered life—to be seen, to be known, to be guided, and to be empowered.

3. Take a few moments to reflect and journal about what a radiant life would look like for you.

CLOSING PRAYER

God of light, fill my life;
Permeate my mind, body, and soul.
God of light, heal my strife;
Redeem my hurts, fill this hole.
God of light, penetrate my darkness;
Light your lamp to all the aching places.
God of light, I long for your closeness;
Guide me and drench my life's spaces.

Day Four

BEGIN WITH THE WORD

Read 1 John 1:5-10

1. In your own words, summarize John's invitation for us.

After John declares that God is light, he offers a clear invitation for his listeners and readers. He wants us to come out of hiding in the dark and choose allegiance to Jesus over and against sin. A life of sin is a life that is antithetical to the teachings of Jesus—it's a life that chooses to live in darkness instead of light, hatred instead of love—it is disobedience against God instead of obedience. He even goes as far as to say that if we claim to be in relationship with God but still choose the darkness, we aren't living in truth. If we try to live in darkness and also light, we aren't living the radiant life. John's invitation for us is, "Come, live in the light; come, live the radiant life."

Often, we think of a life of light as "doing better and avoiding the bad." But that's not actually what John is asking. Think about it this way: when light penetrates, all that is in its path is exposed. Here's another way to put it:

> To walk into the light is to come to terms with who we really are before God—that is, to vulnerably open our whole selves before the penetrating light.

That might sound scary, but we must remember that God is a God of grace and never shame. While light exposes the parts we don't want to have exposed, confession leads us to God's transforming grace. Remember, all of this is about responding to the invitation to radiance.

2. Read verse 9 again. Reflect on what this means for you.

God is a faithfully gracious God and never rejects our confession.

3.   In closing, write a prayer by finishing these sentences:

Gracious God of light, I confess that I . . .

Forgive me for the ways that I have . . .

I thank you for your . . .

Amen.

Day Five

BEGIN WITH A CANDLE

For weekly practices, you will need a lit candle, a quiet room without distractions, and your Bible. Consider finding a place in your home that is the same week after week. Claim it as your holy space—your space to meet with God, hear from God, and commune with God.

Week after week, we will practice grounding prayers which will often include breath prayers, and we will also practice praying the Scriptures. Praying the Scriptures is an ancient tradition used by the earliest Christians. If possible, pray the Scriptures out loud. Praying out loud can be formative for our faith, especially true when praying Scriptures out loud. It might feel awkward at first, but when you do it, remember that you aren't talking to yourself in an empty room. Instead, you are praying to a present God who listens, interacts with us, and forms us in prayer.

Light your candle and place it in front of you. Close your eyes and slowly breathe in and breathe out. As you sit, ask yourself, *What do I hear?* Listen to the sounds in the room and take note. Ask yourself, *What do I smell?* Take a deep breath and note the smells of the space around you. Ask yourself, *What do I feel?* Do you notice the floor beneath you or the chair your back is resting against? Take note of it. Now, ask yourself, *What do I see?* Draw your attention to the candle in front of you. Notice how it flickers and moves about and glows.

You might be wondering, Why are we doing this? Sometimes it can be hard to focus during prayer. We come in with our to-do lists—meals to prep, work to get done, errands to run. Grounding ourselves is a way of helping ourselves get into the present. It is setting aside everything else and being mindful of how we are feeling in this moment. It is also an opportunity to be in the *presence of God.* Repeat the above exercise again if you are still struggling to be in the present and the Presence.

Open your Bible to John 8:12 and read it aloud. Take a few moments to center yourself before the Light of the World by using the candle as a tool. Focus on the candle and take note of the wonder of a flame. A simple spark fanned the flame into light. Take a deep breath in, and as you do, thank God for his light. Exhale slowly and ask God to illuminate your mind in these next few moments. Repeat this until you feel centered and focused before God.

Read the first part of John 8:12 again. This time, read it as a word of praise by replacing the *I* with *you.* "Jesus, you are the light of the world!" Repeat this several times and tell Jesus why his light is so meaningful to you. Repeat "Jesus, you are the light of the world" after each reflection of gratitude.

Now read the second part of John 8:12 again. Read it as a declaration to God by replacing the pronouns with personal pronouns: "Jesus, I will follow you and will never walk in darkness but will have the light of life." Repeat this several times, and ask for Jesus' light to be your source, your energy, your guide, your passion, your focus.

Close with a breath prayer. A breath prayer is an ancient form of prayer that has been practiced for centuries. As you pray, follow the rhythms of your breath for each line.

BREATHE IN, "God of light."

EXHALE, "Illuminate my life."

Repeat this exercise until you feel released from the moment. When you do, extinguish your candle and thank God for his presence.

In the beginning, there was darkness.

Emptiness.

And then . . . A yes.

Not just any yes, but a divine yes, a holy yes, a creative yes.

A yes that spoke and there was permeating light.

Beams and rays and twinkles, so bright.

Yes again, and then darkness was separated from light,
    called night and day.

Then breathed another yes, and there was water and sky
There was dirt in which we grow plants.

And yes, even ants.

And all of creation hushed to hear the Grandest yes of all.

Yes, dear man.
Yes, dear woman.
Yes, always, and forever more.

AN INVITATION TO WALK IN THE LIGHT

GROUP SESSION INTRODUCTION

During our time together, we will focus deeper in on 1 John 2:1-6 and supporting passages. The ultimate invitation throughout this study is to accept the call to live a radiant Christian life. But first, we must be willing to allow the Radiant Light to expose the truth in us.

- Take some time to share highs, lows, and situations where you saw God working during the last week. I like to call this "God glimpses."

- Have someone read out loud all of 1 John 2. As you listen, remember that this is exactly how it would have been received by the recipients of the letter. There would have been a reader, and the church would have sat and listened. As you hear the words, ask the Lord that you would have an open heart and mind to receive these transformative words.

 ## VIDEO
WATCH this week's video.

GROUP DISCUSSION

1. Read aloud 1 John 2:1-2.

John understands that the children of God are prone to sin, and he thus underscores Jesus' advocacy for us through atonement. The biblical concepts of *atonement* are complex ideas found in Scripture. In the Old Testament, purification from one's sins required a "blameless" animal, one without blemish.

2. Look up the following passages and take turns reading them around the circle:

    - Leviticus 1:1-10
    - Leviticus 5:5-10

Throughout Scripture, we see a common theme of God desiring holiness, a life of light. Whenever the people of God were not able to live blameless lives, we see in the Old Testament, God's requirement was to sacrifice an animal without blemish or deformity. These animals were a sacrifice of atonement.

3. Read Romans 3:25. What similarities stand out between the Leviticus and Romans passages?

In the Leviticus passages, we see that the blood of the spotless animal was shed on behalf of the repentant sinner. Now, as Paul declares in Romans and as John tells us here, Jesus is the spotless lamb, the one without blemish, the Radiant One, the Holy God, and the only Righteous One.

4. Read John 1:29 and John 10:11-18.

Because of the faithfulness of the Lamb of God, King Jesus, we are all offered the gift of eternal life. This is a gift available to all, which implies that *we all need it.* What is the personal and corporate impact when we receive this gift?

5. In today's cultural landscape, many have convinced themselves that their *need* for God is minimal. Sin is taken lightly. What are examples of some of the more insidious ways we sin but fail to recognize it as sin?

Now let's zoom out for a moment. When talking about sin, most of us are thinking about it through an individual lens. But evil and sin clearly lurk within the structures and systems of society. Individual sin occurs when individuals normalize behaviors that are antithetical to the ways of God. Structural sin happens when individuals collectively participate in sins that are hurtful or oppressive to the less powerful of society. One example of this kind of sin is slavery. In the case of slavery, individual sin is when a single person treats other human beings as property and not people—whether they own or benefit from the labor of slaves. The structural sin of slavery belongs to all who approve of the practice of slavery, even if they do not directly benefit.

6. What are other examples of structural sin? How might personal sin contribute to structural sin?

All through Scripture, we see Jesus calling us to a way of corporate radiance instead of sin. But as John reminds us, we must begin with the forgiveness that comes through Christ and Christ alone. Forgiveness and a life of radiance only comes one way—through Jesus, the Radiant One.

7. Take a few moments in group silence to consider the ways you have participated in sin that has harmed others. Write them down and then write a prayer asking for forgiveness.

8. Invite one or two to share what they wrote.

CLOSING WORDS

READ the following verse from the hymn "Father, Whose Everlasting Love," from Charles Wesley:

> The world He suffered to redeem;
> For all He hath the atonement made;
> For those that will not come to Him
> The ransom of His Life was paid.

Day 1

BEGIN WITH THE WORD
Read 1 John 2:1-2

In Romans 6:1, the apostle Paul asks, "Shall we go on sinning so that grace may increase?" Similarly, John wants Christians to understand that although forgiveness is a gift for all, the invitation for the Christian life is to not sin. A life of sin impacts the intimate fellowship God offers his people. Of course, John knows that no one will be forever sin free, but the Christian life is one tilted toward the radiance of God and *away* from the sin and brokenness of the world.

Seeing and acknowledging our sin before a radiant God isn't to induce shame; instead, when we are courageously willing to name and acknowledge our sin before God, the power of sin is diminished and the grace of God abundantly increases. There are so many reasons we are afraid to see and acknowledge our sin and brokenness before God. Fear and shame are insidious forces that keep us in hiding because of the belief or fear that we are a bad person, or unlovable, or unwanted. Here is a hint: shame is a liar.

Shame tells us to hide when we are exposed.
Grace tells us to heal when we are exposed.

Shame tells us we will never break free.
Grace gives us a vision for what can be.

Shame tells us God would never accept us as we are.
Grace tells us to come exactly as we are.

Shame was born out of the fall.
Grace was born from the blood of Jesus.

1. In what ways has shame kept you from living a radiant life? In what ways has shame held you back from living in the light of God?

2. In closing, write a courageous prayer of confession. As you write, imagine the grace of God blanketing every word with mercy and love. Remember, "We have an advocate with the Father—Jesus Christ, the Righteous One" (1 John 2:1) Think about it: Jesus, the Radiant One, is advocating for you as you write. And as you write, you are so beautifully being transformed into his radiance.

Day 2

BEGIN WITH THE WORD
Read 1 John 2:3-6

One if the greatest gifts of the Christian life is that God is a God who can *be known*. God is not a distant, unknowable God but one that reveals his heart, character, mind, and love to his very good creation. John urges his readers that the key to knowing God is by walking as Jesus did. In other words, the Christian life is born out of knowing the heart of Jesus. A life that reflects the love of God is born out of walking in the presence and power of the Spirit. A life that reflects the radiance of God is one that knows firsthand the Radiant God.

1. Read John 15:1-17, and as you read, underline or circle in your Bible anytime you see the word *remain* or *abide* or *command*.

2. List below some of the commands Jesus gives to his disciples in this passage.

3. Considering Jesus' commands in John 15, what is some of the fruit of knowing Jesus?

CLOSING PRAYER

Living and loving God,

Thank you that you are a knowable God.

Repeatedly, you reveal your goodness to us.

You show us your love.

You open your heart.

You delight in our knowing.

God, I want to abide in your radiant commands.

May the fruit of knowing you include

Love and joy

Peace and patience

Kindness and goodness

Gentleness and self-control, and

Faithfulness.

Faithfulness when I rise,

Faithfulness when I work.

Faithfulness when I see my neighbor,

And my enemy, too.

God, thank you for your radiant love.

May I not just know about that love, but

May I know it personally.

May my love be born out of your love.

Amen.

Day 3

BEGIN WITH THE WORD
Read 1 John 2:7-11

John writes to his beloved dear friends. As a pastor, he is very concerned about the witness of the church and pushes to consider this through their life together. He writes what he calls an old command, but he then later calls it a new command. So, we are left to wonder, which is it? Old or new? Let's keep this question in mind as we read on.

1. Read Leviticus 19:18. After reading this, what is the connection between John's command and the one in Leviticus?

2. Read John 13:34-35. We might be wondering: If this is a command written in the book of Leviticus before Jesus ever uttered these words on earth, why would he now be calling it a new command?

We can conclude that Jesus calls this a new command because *love is fully realized in the life, teachings, death, and resurrection of Jesus.* In other words, love is fully embodied in Jesus to the fullest. What John wants us to now consider is if this same love is *fully realized* in us.

READ 1 John 2:8.

In John's letter, we are reminded that light (and love!) is realized in Jesus, and for those who live in Jesus, this same light (and love!) is realized in us.

3. When and where does love radiate out of my life? When and where does love radiate out of my church?

It sounds like an old, pithy saying these days: "They will know we are Christians by our love." But perhaps we need to reflect on this more than ever.

4. In closing, write a prayer for yourself, your family, and
   your church community by finishing these sentences:

Dear radiant and loving Lord,

I thank you for your radiant . . .

*I pray that my church community would reflect your
    radiant love by . . .*

I pray that my life would reflect your radiant love by . . .

Amen.

Day 4

BEGIN WITH THE WORD
Read 1 John 2:15-17

There is so much to love about God's good and beautiful world. It is to be enjoyed and stewarded with care. The word that John is using for "world"—*kosmos*—has a different meaning than what we know as God's good and beautiful creation. For John, *kosmos* is a picture of those who live in direct rebellion against God. Jesus experienced this during his earthly ministry by those who were in opposition to his exhortations and teachings. And now, John is warning the Christians in Asia Minor to not live as those who live in rebellion against God. Those who belong to God are to live in a way that reflects the heart of God's kingdom, not the heart of the world. Loving God and living worldly lives are incompatible.

In Jesus' Sermon on the Mount, he gives us a vision for the antithesis of worldly living.

1. Read Matthew 5:21-48. Make a list of things Jesus might say "worldly" people do.

At the conclusion of Matthew 5, Jesus calls us to be perfect as our heavenly Father is perfect. We can almost hear echoes of these words in John's plea when he says, "Whoever does the will of God lives forever" (1 John 2:17). Both Jesus and John are calling Christians to live as ones who belong to God. And both of these passages are also couched in a lesson of learning to love as God loves.

2. Read Matthew 5:43-48 again. Read 1 John 2:9-11 again. What do these passages have in common?

We can conclude, then, that the way of Christian perfection and eternal life is the way of learning to love as God loves. Learning to love as God loves—indiscriminate love, countercultural love, boundary-breaking love, and crosscultural love.

3. Who in your life has been hard to love? In closing, write down the name of a person who has been hard to love. Write their name on a note card and place it somewhere that is visible every day. Every time you see the note, pray for them.

Day 5

BEGIN WITH A CANDLE

Light your candle and place it in front of you. Find a comfortable place to sit.

Close your eyes and slowly breathe in and breathe out. As you sit, ask yourself, *What do I hear?* Listen to the sounds in the room and take note. Ask yourself, *What do I smell?* Take a deep breath and note the smells of the space around you. Ask yourself, *What do I feel?* Do you notice the floor beneath you or the chair your back is resting against? Take note of it. Now, ask yourself, *What do I see?* Draw your attention to the candle in front of you. Notice how it flickers and moves about and glows. Take mental note of the wonder of a flame. A simple spark fanned the flame into light. Take a deep breath in, and as you do, thank God for his light. Exhale slowly and ask God to illuminate your mind in these next few moments. Repeat this until you are in the present and the Presence.

Open your Bible and read Psalm 17:1-8 out loud. Now pause and be still before God. Thank God for his very good presence. Stay silent before God, listening for his voice. Listen for words that are echoing in your mind, perhaps from the Scripture.

Read Psalm 17:1-8 out loud again. As you recite it, let it not just be words from a page, but let them now flow from your heart to God's heart.

Now pause again and be still before God. What words or phrases are impressed on your heart from the passage just prayed? Let's focus on them for a moment. Look in the passage for where that word or phrase might be written. Recite it again as a prayer to God.

Repeat this exercise until you feel released from the moment. When you do, extinguish your candle and thank God for his presence.

You call me to walk from
   darkness to light,
From dark crevices to holy life.
Your banner is brilliance,
   your ways are upright.
You call me to mediate
   your goodness,

To join you in setting a weary
   world right.
Impel me by your power, propel
   me by your fullness.
"Here am I, Lord, send me."

AN INVITATION TO HOLY LIGHT

GROUP SESSION INTRODUCTION

This week, we will lean in to our relationship status with God. We have a seat at God's table as the family of God.

- Begin by sharing highs, lows, and God glimpses from the week.
- There are different ways we communicate our relationship status with other people. I remember in the mid-2000s hearing someone remark, "A relationship isn't official unless it's Facebook official!" We communicate relationship status through social media channels and through wedding rings. What are other ways we communicate relationships today?
- Have someone read out loud all of 1 John 3 and 4. As you listen, remember that this is exactly how it would have been received by the recipients of the letter. There would have been a reader and the church would have sat and listened. As you hear the words, ask the Lord that you would have an open heart and mind to receive these transformative words.

VIDEO

WATCH this week's video.

GROUP DISCUSSION

In John's letter, he defines the relationship for all believers.

1. Read 1 John 3:1-3. How does John define the relationship
    that Christians have with God?

Think for a moment about a child and an adoring parent. Think about
the relationship and how they interact with one another.

2. What is the child's role and what is the parent's role in
    the relationship? How might God's role be similar to the
    parent's role? Reread verses 2-3.

John wants the Christian to understand that as children of God, we will one day be like the resurrected Jesus. One day we will be made whole, holy, and pure. This is the hope that we can hold on to. But John isn't only interested in our relationship with God in the future, he is also very interested in the present lives of God's children.

3. Read 1 John 3:4-10. What are John's warnings for the children of God?

At first glance, it might seem like verses 1-3 and then 4-10 are totally unrelated. However, for John the familial theme ties the entire passage together. Have you ever seen a child imitate their parent? As God's children, we are to live in the way of God—the way of wholeness, purity, and holiness. We are to imitate God.

4. Reread verse 9. What is the antithesis to living as a child of God?

"Seed" in this verse is another way of referring to the Holy Spirit. When we are born of God, the Spirit is alive in us and propels us toward the ways of God and away from the brokenness of the world. John isn't calling us toward sinless perfection; instead, John believes that we will either have a propensity toward God or we will have a propensity toward sin. We can't be tilted toward both. We run toward God at the same time we run away from sin.

5. Describe a community of believers that is marked by those who seek and turn to the Father again and again. Describe what it looks like when a community reflects the world's brokenness.

6. Read 1 John 3:1. The life of holiness, wholeness, and purity that we are called to live as God's children flows out of the reality that God loved us first. Take a few moments for that to soak in.

You

Are

Beloved.

Henri Nouwen says it best in *Life of the Beloved*: "We are intimately loved long before our parents, teachers, spouses, children and friends loved or wounded us. That's the truth of our lives. That's the truth I want you to claim for yourself. That's the truth spoken by the voice that says, 'You are my Beloved.'"

CLOSING WORDS

Go around the group one at a time and say out loud, "I am beloved." And after one person says it, respond as a group, "You are beloved." Then go on to the next person—"I am beloved"—and respond as a group, "You are beloved."

Ask someone to close in prayer.

Day 1

BEGIN WITH THE WORD
Read 1 John 3:1-10

Continuing with the familial theme from our group time, let's now consider the ways being a child of God affects our relationships with our friends, families, neighbors, and even strangers. The big question to ponder today is: *Do they know we are God's children?* Not because we tell them but because of our actions. Do they see Jesus in us? Do our enemies know that we are children of God because of the love of God alive in us?

1. Take a few minutes to reflect on a recent interaction with someone who offended you, when you responded in ways you aren't proud of. Journal about the interaction and how you responded.

Throughout this entire passage, John has been underscoring the criticality of living as God's children with the fruit of holiness. When we remain in Christ—that is, when we continue a life fully surrendered—we are transformed into the life of holiness. When we don't remain in Christ—when we live a life in defiance to Jesus—our life will reflect the decay and brokenness of this world. Sin within the context of John's letter is when one lives in direct defiance of the ways of God. If we are truly born of God, we won't live in defiance of the ways of God, says John.

It isn't that Christians live lives of total "Christian perfection." Instead, John is calling Christians to live surrendered lives day by day, minute by minute, second by second, moment by moment, and breath by breath. There are days, seconds, and moments that our posture of surrender turns into defiance of the ways of God. This is often played out in our relationships and shows up in bitterness, rage, gossip, malice, and deceit.

2. Return to your reflection from above. Challenging rela-
    tionships can sometimes be the greatest place where
    our Christian lives are put to test. Below, write a prayer
    surrendering to God these difficult relationships, and
    ask God to form you into his likeness—as his child.

Day 2

BEGIN WITH THE WORD

Read Genesis 4:1-16

1. What were the prevailing sins of Cain that led to the murder of his brother?

2. Read 1 John 3:11-24. According to John, what was at the root of Cain's murder of his brother?

John uses a tragic illustration of some of the earliest-known effects of sin and brokenness by pointing to the Bible's first murder. John foreshadows the looming persecution that the early church would experience, while highlighting that murder and hatred are a mark of the evil one. But in verses 14-16, he reminds us that as God's children, we are to rise above the hatred of this world by loving as Jesus loved us. Cain is an example of those who remain in the sin, decay, and brokenness of this world: the supreme example of Jesus is the example of the way of love we are to live as God's children.

As we reflected in the reading from day one, living in community is often a true test of our willingness to remain in the power of Christ. Jesus' example should stretch the will and imagination of any Christian. Jesus not only laid down his life for those who loved him, but he laid down his life for those who *hated* him. John pushes us to have the same posture as Jesus—that is, love-drenched action toward those who are difficult to love.

3. Make a list of the kinds of people that you find difficult to love (be honest!):

Remember the words of John—love without action is meaningless.

4. Now, make a list of love-drenched-action steps you can take toward those people who are difficult to love:

CLOSING PRAYER

Lord, I confess that more hard-to-love people come to mind than love-drenched action items. I confess that my propensity to hate like Cain is all too often a reality. Lord, I want to live like you, love like you, lay down my life like you. Shift my heart away from hatred and drench it with your all-consuming love. Help me to love subversively. Help me to love in the face of evil. Help me to love in the face of hatred. Help me to love counter-culturally. Help me to love even when I don't want to. Help me to love without boundaries. Fill my imagination day in and day out of what love-drenched action looks like. Amen.

Day 3

BEGIN WITH THE WORD

Read 1 John 4:1-6

John pastorally warns the fellowship of believers to be aware of those at risk of swaying the people of God away from Christ. He doesn't want the people to be blindly led astray—as we are all at risk of such a thing! Instead, he wants the fellowship to test, discern, and be sure that the teachers and prophets are indeed from God.

1. John wants the Christian to understand that there are two kinds of spirits in this world. What are they?

These false teachers were creating fragmentations within the early church; thus, the witness of the church was at risk. There were frauds working to disrupt the unity.

2. Read Jesus' prayer in John 17:23-26. What is at stake if the unity of believers is disrupted?

This unity was disrupted when false teachers influenced the people of God away from the Spirit-inspired message.

3. John says we must test teachers with two tests.

■ Read John 17:2-3. What is the first test?

■ Read John 17:4-6. What is the second test?

Antichrist is a word that is used in many spaces, in many generations, for many reasons. Every presidential election cycle, I hear—more than once—about any of the candidates, "He/she is the antichrist!" When I was younger, I knew that this was a bad thing, but back then I fearfully assumed it meant doom and gloom and that the obliteration of the world was looming. But this is not how John is using the term. An *antichrist* is anyone who lives or teaches in direct opposition to the ways of Jesus. There are *many* antichrists in our world today. Now, like then, we must be wise and discerning. The best tests, according to John, are to test what they say about Jesus and to test what the world says about them.

CLOSING PRAYER

Lord, as one member of the body of Christ, I want to lean into the vision of unity and oneness that you prayed for in the Garden of Gethsemane. Help me to live, lead, and teach your truth, and help me to discern and test when I'm not living and leading and teaching your truth. Help me to also test and discern when there are teachers who are not representing you and your truth. Help us—your church—to be one just as you and the Father are one. Lord, may the world know your truth through our unity and our witness. Amen.

Day 4

BEGIN WITH THE WORD

Read 1 John 4:7-21

1. John's exhortation to love continues in John 4. But now he tells us the very origin and source of love. What is it?

While John's appeal to have love-drenched action continues, he pastorally wants his "dear friends" to know the foundation to living this out. In his commentary on John, New Testament scholar I. Howard Marshall asks the important question whether it is possible to love as a non-Christian. He answers it this way:

> There is love outside the Christian church, and sometimes non-Christians seem to love one another better than Christians do. How is the existence of such love to be explained, and what does its presence indicate regarding the status before God of those who show it? Has John been shutting his eyes to the facts of life?

He then reminds us of a helpful theological framework that exists within the doctrine of creation. He goes on:

> It is because men are created in the image of God, an image which has been defaced but not destroyed by the Fall, that they still have the capacity to love.

Marshall, then, reminds us that we all fall short of love-drenched action without the power of God. We are all marked by the brokenness of the world, but when we walk in the grace, truth, and abundant power of God, we are impelled and propelled to love-drenched action.

Not only are we moved to action, but God's love grounds us and undergirds our lives.

2. Read verse 18 again. As you read, consider this question: How might God be calling you to live a love-drenched life?

When God's love matures and grows within us, love is incompatible with fear. In his commentary on the letters of John, Gary M. Burge reminds us that "fear and love are mutually exclusive." Many scholars agree that the kind of "fear" that John is getting at is both related to the future judgment and the present reality. When we are grounded in the love of God, and when it grows and matures in us, we can navigate life with humility-drenched confidence before God and others.

3. Write a prayer below asking for God to be your center, your foundation, and your source for love-drenched action as well as humility-drenched confidence.

Day 5

BEGIN WITH A CANDLE

Light your candle and place it in front of you. Find a comfortable place to sit.

Close your eyes and slowly breathe in and breathe out. As you sit, ask yourself, *What do I hear?* Listen to the sounds in the room and take note. Ask yourself, *What do I smell?* Take a deep breath and note the smells of the space around you. Ask yourself, *What do I feel?* Do you notice the floor beneath you or the chair your back is resting against? Take note of it. Now, ask yourself, *What do I see?* Draw your attention to the candle in front of you. Notice how it flickers and moves about and glows. Take mental note of the wonder of a flame. A simple spark fanned the flame into light. Take a deep breath in, and as you do, thank God for his light. Exhale slowly and ask God to illuminate your mind in these next few moments. Repeat this until you are in the present and the Presence.

Open your Bible and read John 9:1-41 out loud. There's a lot to read, but take your time. As you read, imagine the scene.

Now pause and be still before God. Thank God for his very good presence. Stay silent before God, listening for his voice. Listen for words that are echoing in your mind, perhaps from the Scripture.

Read John 9:35-41 out loud again. Now pause again and be still before God. What words or phrases are impressed on your heart from the passage just prayed? Or *who* in the story stands out to you? Who are you in the story? Finding ourselves in the story can be a way of getting in touch with our own longings before God and sometimes even our own sinfulness before a gracious God. What might God be calling you to do?

Pause again and be still before God.

Slowly **BREATHE IN**, "God, I want to see."

Slowly **EXHALE**, "Illuminate my eyes."

Slowly **BREATHE IN**, "God, shine your light in my darkness."

Slowly **EXHALE**, "Drench me in your light."

Repeat this exercise until you feel released from the moment. When you do, extinguish your candle and thank God for his presence.

THE WORLD WILL ALWAYS ASK,
When will the light come,
As we spin in never ending darkness?
Creation groans, war rages regardless

But there in the wilderness,
A sign of spring.
Uprooting the seed of bitterness,
Holy mischief rings.

From the cup of suffering,
 Hope and light reign.
A plan from the beginning,
 Healing from our pain.

The world will want to know,
When will the church rise?
Will she live the justice she's
 been preaching?
Will she believe the words
 He's been teaching?

But there with the despairing,
A gleam of light.
The Bride is pregnant,
 bearing witness,
Setting the world to right.

They will know we love Jesus
Not just by our words
When His Kingdom comes in us
And when our actions are heard.

LOVE-DRENCHED LIFE

GROUP SESSION INTRODUCTION

This week we will reflect on our collective calling to live a life totally drenched and propelled by the love of God. Listen for John's pastoral call to us.

- Open with highs, lows, and God glimpses from the week.

- What are some general examples of something that love *does?* (Love is compassionate.) What are things that love *doesn't do?* (Love is not hateful.)

- This week, we will see John's continued pastoral call to live a love-drenched life—that is, a life that is living out the abundance of God's love and therefore is propelled to go and do likewise. To open our time together, share examples of where you've seen this lived out this week or when you've seen love embodied in a community.

- Have someone read out loud all of 1 John 5. As you listen, remember that this is exactly how it would have been received by the recipients of the letter. There would have been a reader, and the church would have sat and listened. As you hear the words, ask the Lord to give open hearts and minds to receive these transformative words.

VIDEO

WATCH this week's video.

GROUP DISCUSSION

Up until now, we have been able to decipher that a theological debate has erupted in the church. We've read about false accusations and warnings about false prophets and antichrists. Scholars have laid out the possibilities of what some of these debates might have been, and Gary M. Burge, in his commentary, puts it this way: "Teachers and prophets were making pronouncements about truth, some of whom claimed to be inspired by the Spirit. But they were interpreting Christ's work so that the cross was secondary (or irrelevant), and they were promoting alternate sources of 'life' that had no need of Christ's substitutionary death."

John wants nothing more than for the church to walk in the way of Jesus with a love-drenched-action-oriented life. In his concluding remarks, he continues to underscore this while reminding them of the continued dichotomies of sin and light, and evil and life. His final words almost seem abrupt.

1. Read verse 21.

Some scholars say that verse 21 might very well be the point of the whole of the letter. Ultimately, idolatry is anything that tugs the people of God away from the truth and supremacy of Jesus. Let's spend the rest of our time now zooming out and looking at idolatrous temptations in today's world.

2. If idolatry is anything that tugs us away from the truth and supremacy of Jesus, where do you see this prevalent in our culture today? Think of specific examples of idolatry.

3. Are any of these idols more insidious and hidden even within our own churches? If so, what are they?

It's often easier to think of how *other people* worship idols, and not so much ourselves. Let's spend time taking an inventory.

4. Have the leader read the following questions out loud with everyone's eyes closed. As the leader reads, be honest with yourself and try to be open to the truth of these questions.

    ■ What do you spend most of your time doing?

    ■ Where does the majority of your money go?

■ What do you fear losing (besides loved ones)?

■ What is your "if only"? "If only I had_____"

■ What has control over your life?

■ What is inhibiting you from living in the light of Christ?

5. Open your eyes. Reflect quietly on the specific things
   that convicted you as the questions were being read.

Idols make so many false promises—they promise contentment, ful-
fillment, meaning, and purpose. But in the end, we often find ourselves
wanting more.

6. In what ways have you experienced this with specific
   idols?

7. Let's get personal for a moment. We all have "pet idols" that lure and tempt us more than others. Would you be willing to name these out loud?

8. Now, let's remember some of John's pleas in the five chapters of this letter. What are ways John believes we can walk in the truth of Jesus and avoid idolatry?

CLOSING PRAYER

In closing, pray for the person to your left, that they would be able to walk in the truth and supremacy of King Jesus.

Day 1

BEGIN WITH THE WORD

Read 1 John 5:1-5

1. John reminds us again of a criterion for being born of God in verse 1. What is it?

2. Read verse 2 again. John lays out the second criterion for being born of God. What is it?

3. Read verse 3 again. John lays out the third criterion for being born of God. What is it?

4. John makes a stunning declaration in verses 4 and 5. Did you catch it? Read it again and write it below.

"Overcoming the world" almost sounds heroic, doesn't it? But John isn't talking about a heroic conquering; instead, he's talking about living the kind of life that lives and walks in the abundance of God's love and resists the ways of this world. Remember, in John's letter, "the world" represents anyone who lives in direct opposition to the ways of God. To overcome isn't to conquer those who live in opposition to God but instead to walk in the love of God with a love-drenched-action-oriented life.

5. What are specific areas of your life in which you are walking in the love of God?

CLOSING PRAYER

Jesus, the victory is yours. You overcame sin and death, and you lived a life that rose above the decaying, deceitful, and death-filled world. I confess that there are days when my propensity points toward these realities instead of you. But Jesus, I want to walk in the power of your victory. I want to walk in the abundance of your freedom. I want to walk in your truth and light. Jesus, there are areas in my life where I am longing for victory. You know them, I have named them, and now I confess them to you. I ask that in the power of your grace, you would help me live in freedom. Set me free from the broken nature that reigns over me and help me live a life that looks like you. Amen.

Day 2

BEGIN WITH THE WORD

Read 1 John 5:6-12

Scholars agree that this is one of the more peculiar passages in John's letter. We are left making our best contextual conclusion as to what John means by "water and blood." Some have wondered if John is referring to the Eucharist, while others wonder if it is baptism and the cross. Either way, John says that Jesus has come *through* water and blood. Again, this leaves us wondering what John means by "coming." Is it Jesus' coming into his public ministry? Is it his second coming? Constantine Campbell concludes in his commentary:

> The water and blood signify Jesus's baptism and death. Through [this], Jesus *comes*—he enters ministry through baptism, and he enters his role as Savior through death. He not only ministered (water) but came through baptism *and death* (blood). The water and blood testify that Jesus came to serve and die for humanity, while the Spirit testifies that he is God's divine Son.

The religious leaders of John's time had a vested interest in Jesus. Many religious leaders were making false proclamations of truth that were not inspired by the Holy Spirit. The cross became secondary with many of these false teachers.

As Christians, our discernment practices put our witness at stake. In other words, when we aren't discerning of who is teaching and leading us, we are at risk of being led astray. As children of God, we must cling to the witness of Jesus that comes from God. When we do, we are receiving eternal life.

1. Make a list of areas in your life where you need more wisdom.

2. Spend time asking God to give you wisdom in these areas.

Day 3

BEGIN WITH THE WORD

Read 1 John 5:13-15

John now tells us why he writes this letter with such rich theological proclamations.

1.   What is his reasoning and why does it matter?

Verse 14 is packed with the very good news that God desires our closeness and wants to hear our longings. Not only does God desire it, but we don't have to be afraid to bring God our requests. When we come, God hears us. If you're like me, you are already thinking about the prayer requests that haven't been answered in ways you had hoped.

2.   Let's take a look at Jesus' prayer in the Garden of Geth-semane. Read Mark 14:32-36.

It wasn't that God the Father turned an ear or hardened his heart. Instead, God heard the plea of the suffering Jesus. Jesus' aches were welcome in the arms of his Father. But read again the final sentence of verse 36:

Yet not what I will, but what you will.

Jesus resolves that it is ultimately the will of the Father that has supremacy, not his own will. Now you might be wondering, So why even pray at all?

Prayer is all too often thought of as pulling a lever so the results *I* want will be delivered by God. But prayer is more about formation than it is a delivery system. In prayer, God hears us, welcomes us, and forms us. In prayer, our own will is shaped, our ideas are formed, our passions are aligned with God's passions, and our aches are replaced with peace.

3. Let's put this into practice. Surely even now you have your own aches, longings, and requests. Take a few moments of silence. Then go to God in prayer, making your request. Acknowledge that you trust that God hears you and receives your request. And then conclude your

Day 4

BEGIN WITH THE WORD

Read 1 John 5:16-21

Again, John wants us to understand the pathway for those who are not born of God. Those who are born of God understand the seriousness of sin.

1. After John reminds us that we can trust in the God who hears our prayers, who and what does he ask us to pray for?

2. John is specific about the sin he's referring to. What are the two kinds of sin he's referring to?

The Old Testament may be a helpful place for us to dig deeper on these two kinds of sin.

3. Read the following passages and do your best to describe what these sins have in common.

■ Leviticus 4:2-27; 5:15-18 ; Numbers 15:27-31; Psalm 19:13

4. Now read the following passages and again do your best to describe what these sins have in common.

- Numbers 15:30-31 ; Deuteronomy 17:12

The latter passages likely seem severe, but the juxtaposition of the two kinds of sin that John describes is important. There are some sins that are unintentional, and there are others that are willfully disobedient to the ways of God—this is the kind that he says leads to death. Those who commit the sins that lead to death do not believe in God's ways and intentionally choose not to walk in the grace of God. They refuse to receive the forgiveness of God and *choose* to walk in the ways of sin, death, decay, and brokenness. John does, however, encourage us to pray for those who believe and have received the grace of God but *struggle* to walk in the way. We ought to pray for them so that our fellowship and witness is strengthened.

5. Spend time making a list of people to pray for. Remember, when you pray for those who might be struggling, try not to be haughty or even gossipy. Jesus reminds us in his Sermon on the Mount to also remember that we are sinners! Pray so that the witness of the church is strengthened.

Day 5

BEGIN WITH A CANDLE

Light your candle and place it in front of you. Find a comfortable place to sit.

Close your eyes and slowly breathe in and breathe out. As you sit, ask yourself, *What do I hear?* Listen to the sounds in the room and take note. Ask yourself, *What do I smell?* Take a deep breath and note the smells of the space around you. Ask yourself, *What do I feel?* Do you notice the floor beneath you or the chair your back is resting against? Take note of it. Now, ask yourself, *What do I see?* Draw your attention to the candle in front of you. Notice how it flickers and moves about and glows. Take mental note of the wonder of a flame. A simple spark fanned the flame into light. Take a deep breath in, and as you do, thank God for his light. Exhale slowly and ask God to luminate your mind in these next few moments. Repeat this until you are in the present and the Presence.

Open your Bible and read all of Psalm 32 out loud. Now pause and be still before God. Thank God for his very good presence. Stay silent before God, listening for his voice. Listen for words that are echoing in your mind, perhaps from the Scripture.

Read Psalm 32 out loud again. As you recite it, let it not just be words from a page, but let them now flow from your heart to God's heart.

Now pause again and be still before God. What words or phrases are impressed on your heart from the passage just prayed? Let's focus on them for a moment. Look in the passage for where that word or phrase might be written. Recite it again as a prayer to God.

Repeat this exercise until you feel released from the moment. When you do, extinguish your candle and thank God for his presence.

In Christ's light, we stay,
Guided on the righteous way,
His love leads our day.

REMAINING IN THE LIGHT OF CHRIST

GROUP SESSION INTRODUCTION

This week, we will reflect on what it means to embody the light of Christ. John calls us to live in the light and reflect the light in a dark and hurting world.

- Open with highs, lows, and God glimpses from the week.
- Have someone read out loud all of 2 John. As you listen, remember that this is exactly how it would have been received by the recipients of the letter. There would have been a reader, and the church would have sat and listened. As you hear the words, ask the Lord that you would have an open heart and mind to receive these transformative words.

VIDEO
WATCH this week's video.

GROUP DISCUSSION

As we read in 1 John, God is the standard of love, the source of love, the essence of love, and God *is* love. Through the faithfulness of the life, teachings, death, resurrection, and ascension of King Jesus, the love of God has been revealed to us. As God's children, we are to live likewise. This is a repeated theme in John's letters.

96   WEEK 5—REMAINING IN THE LIGHT OF CHRIST

1. In what verse is God's love once again underscored?

    ■ In verses 4-6, John wants us to live in _____.

    ■ In verses 7-11, John wants us to live in _____.

2. What are the warnings in 2 John 7-11?

3. How might these warnings be relevant for us today?

John's warning about welcoming the wicked isn't so much about welcoming anyone who walks in the way of sin; John is specifically talking about those who claim to be teachers of Jesus but instead lead people astray from the ways of Jesus.

4. As in his previous letter, John is concerned about truth. Read the following passages and write next to each one the source of truth John describes.

■ 1 John 2:20

■ John 14:18

■ John 15:26

■ John 16:13

5. Now read the following passages and write next to each one what truth *does*.

    ■ 1 John 1:6

    ■ John 3:21

■ John 8:32

■ John 14:15-17

■ John 15:10-14

6. After reading these passages, in what ways do you see truth prevalent in your church? In what ways do you see the "false truth"?

Discerning truth can be tricky, especially in a world where everyone wants to claim their own truth—"to each their own." But discerning truth and life must be the work of the community. It takes time, prayer, wisdom, and sages among us. While it's tempting to read passages like this and become haughty by listing out all the "bad actors" out there, instead we can hold up a mirror and ask God to show us how we have misrepresented Jesus.

7. If you are willing, share in the group ways that we are prone to misrepresent Jesus.

CLOSING PRAYER

Close in prayer by praying for one another. Pray that we would all walk in the light of Christ in our daily lives.

Day 1

BEGIN WITH THE WORD
Read 2 John 1-3

The author of the letter doesn't immediately state his personal name. Most scholars agree that the elder mentioned here is the same person who wrote the earlier letter that we know as 1 John. When I served as the lead pastor at a church in Southern California, I wrote a weekly email that was called "From the Pastor's Heart." It was a personal "in-house" email where I could nurture the church through my writing. John calling himself "the elder" establishes him in a pastoral or even shepherding role. I. Howard Marshall notes that this term gave John "affectionate reverence as 'the old man.'" John's first letter served as a theological letter for the public church, while this second letter is more personal.

1. To whom does he write this letter?

The way he addresses the church is another way of saying "the church and its members." Calling the church "lady" might have been similar to understanding the church in the feminine as "the bride of Christ."

2. Read the following passages and describe what truth
    reveals.

    ■ 1 John 1:8

    ■ John 1:14

    ■ John 16:13

    ■ John 17:17, 19

We've only touched the tip of the iceberg with the multiple layers of truth. We as the people of God are not the source of truth, as we've read. Truth is sourced through the fellowship of the Trinity, and it is revealed not by us but by God. Thus, we must be careful not to weaponize truth as a barrier or dividing line between one another. It must be discerned carefully and lovingly.

In other words, our pursuit of truth must always be drenched in love and grace and mercy. While we must pursue it, we don't own it; rather, we humbly seek to understand it as God lovingly reveals it to us. Let us not become haughty in our longing for truth.

CLOSING PRAYER

Lord, we fall on our knees and confess that our minds fall short of knowing and understanding your fully glorified truth. And yet, we long for it— more of it—to see, to know, to live, and to experience your transforming truth that propels us to live as children of light. God, we seek you with our whole hearts, not so we can draw lines in the sand against our neighbor but so we can reflect your truth and love amid a weary world. God of truth, enlighten us. God of truth, show us the way. God of truth, increase our wisdom. God of truth, shine your light in the dark crevices of our hearts, in our communities, and in our worlds. God of truth, may your radiant light burst in the corners of our world full of pain, hurt, and brokenness, and may your truth be revealed so that every tongue confesses that you are the Lord and source of all truth. Amen.

Day 2

BEGIN WITH THE WORD
Read 2 John 4-6

John repeats perhaps his most favorite command: Love one another. He acknowledges that this is not a new command, but one that we have heard from the beginning of Jesus' ministry and one that we must continue to press into. While we have spent a lot of time unpacking the command to love one another, it is important that we to continue to press into this with passion. Marianne Meye Thompson, in her commentary on John, describes this love for us:

> We show that we love God when we do what God desires, and what God desires is that we live a life of love. Love is not a feeling or emotion, but a way of life that manifests itself concretely in its concern for others in obedience to the commandments of God. Love circumscribes the whole of life and ought to permeate the actions and attitudes of the Christian person.

Love must be lived. Done. Given. Let's check in with how we are doing with living the love-drenched-action-oriented life that both John and Jesus call us to live.

1. In what ways have you demonstrated love-drenched action?

2. In what ways have you not demonstrated love-drenched
    action?

3. Complete these prayers for yourself:

    ■ *God, I confess that I sometimes fall short . . .*

■ *God, fill my life with . . .*

■ *God, show me the way of love by . . .*

■ *God, strengthen me by . . .*

Day 3

BEGIN WITH THE WORD

Read 2 John 7-10

John's pastoral concern is revealed in verse 7. There is a toxic threat to the fledgling community, and he wants them to remain vigilant. The toxic threat is in direct opposition to the truth he described in the previous verses.

1.   What is the main problem with the deceivers as described in verse 7?

John understands what is at stake when the truth of Jesus is challenged. To abandon truth is to "lose" what the community has worked for—that is, life. To walk away from truth is to walk away from life. He cautions the early church to be aware of teachings that are in direct opposition to the life, light, and truth of Jesus.

It might seem harsh, but the refusal to welcome a deceiver in a house was more than just refusing a seat at a dinner table, because houses were house *churches*. John didn't want their influence infiltrating the community. When the church welcomes the deceivers in, they are "sharing in the wicked work." He didn't want the early church to be swayed into compromising their theological foundations.

2. In what ways have you observed pockets of the church compromising our core beliefs?

3. In what areas of your life are you struggling to trust the
   Source of Truth?

4. In closing, write a prayer asking God to give you eyes
   to see his truth and wisdom to discern when there are
   "deceivers."

Day 4

BEGIN WITH THE WORD
Read 2 John 12-13

1. What is the desired outcome of John visiting the community face to face?

John's vision for the Christian life was about a holy *people* who together live under the lordship of King Jesus. It was never about an individual and Jesus; it was about *people* and Jesus—a holy *we*, not a holy *me*. So, when John says, "so that our joy may be complete," he is talking about the kind of joy that is received, given, shared, and experienced within the fellowship. The longing for joy is at last fulfilled when God's people are all together.

In a society that offers millions of means to enhance the Christian life through technology, it's easy enough to be tempted to do the Christian life alone. But the solo Christian life would have made no sense to the early church—it was, and always is, about a holy *we*, not a holy *me*.

Did you know that you have strengths and gifts to help make the "joy complete" for others around you? Maybe you're a teacher. Or maybe you have the gift of faith. Or maybe you have the gift of hospitality. Or maybe it's the gift of simply being present when others need it.

2. Sometimes we can identify our gifts by acknowledging things that we love doing. Using our gifts brings us joy! What do you most enjoy doing?

3. What's one way that your gifts could be used to enhance the joy of your local church?

4. Write a prayer asking God to help you be a faithful steward of the gifts that God has given. Ask God to stretch you and grow you so that the people around you will experience the joy of the gifts given.

Day 5

BEGIN WITH A CANDLE

Light your candle and place it in front of you. Find a comfortable place to sit.

Close your eyes and slowly breathe in and breathe out. As you sit, ask yourself, *What do I hear?* Listen to the sounds in the room and take note. Ask yourself, *What do I smell?* Take a deep breath and note the smells of the space around you. Ask yourself, *What do I feel?* Do you notice the floor beneath you or the chair your back is resting against? Take note of it. Now, ask yourself, *What do I see?* Draw your attention to the candle in front of you. Notice how it flickers and moves about and glows. Take mental note of the wonder of a flame. A simple spark fanned the flame into light. Take a deep breath in, and as you do, thank God for his light. Exhale slowly and ask God to illuminate your mind in these next few moments. Repeat this until you are in the present and the Presence.

Open your Bible and read all of John 17 out loud. Now pause and be still before God. Thank God for his very good presence. Stay silent before God, listening for his voice. Listen for words that are echoing in your mind, perhaps from the Scripture.

Read Psalm 17 out loud again. Let it not just be words from a page, but let them now flow from your heart to God's heart

Now pause again and be still before God. Pay attention to the yearnings that align with the yearnings of Jesus' prayer. Let's focus on them for a moment. Look in the passage for where that yearning is reflected. Recite it again as your own prayer to God.

Repeat this exercise until you feel released from the moment. When you do, extinguish your candle and thank God for his presence.

I ONCE THOUGHT MY FAITH WAS
Private and personal.
I'd climb to the heavens—
Solo and vertical.

Say prayers in the morning
Quiet and alone.
Grow like a mighty tree
But solo and unknown.

But one bright dawn, I saw
My roots were intertwined
With your roots and mine
And our grandparents' combined.

The forest was singing,
Piercing through the
Darkness,
"I need you, you need me,
    we need you, you need us."

AN INVITATION TO GLOWING COMMUNITY

GROUP SESSION INTRODUCTION

Our collective call as God's people is to reflect the light of God as a *people in community.* This week, we will discover what it means to corporately reflect the light of God.

- Share highs, lows, and God glimpses from the week.
- Have someone read out loud all of 3 John.

As you listen, remember that this is exactly how it would have been received by the recipients of the letter. There would have been a reader, and the church would have sat and listened. As you hear the words, ask the Lord for open hearts and minds to receive these transformative words.

VIDEO

WATCH this week's video.

GROUP DISCUSSION

The third letter of John describes three different people with different kinds of character. Take some time to describe the differences between the three.

1. How does John describe Gaius?

2. How does John describe Diotrephes?

3. How does John describe Demetrius?

These three men have their names written in ink for three different reasons. Two knew the truth and walked in it, and one did not. We have access to the truth, and it is revealed to us. Walking in the truth is the invitation for all Christians. The question for us is, What kind of legacy will we leave? What kind of impact will our church have? How do you want to be remembered?

When we think about how we want to be remembered one day, we mostly think about our own personal legacy. But our collective witness is at stake. John wrote so prolifically to the early church because he cared about their collective witness. Take a few moments and reflect on the witness of the church today.

4. How will the church be remembered generations from now?

5. What can we do *now* to strengthen the witness of the church?

CLOSING PRAYER

Close in prayer by praying for our collective witness. Do this by taking turns lifting up a one- or two-sentence prayer and then follow by responding as a group, "Lord, hear our prayer." For example:

Individual: "Lord, I pray for healing in our nation."

Group: "Lord, hear our prayer."

- Pray for the witness of the church in all the ways we engage in political issues.
- Pray for the witness of the church in the ways we engage in social issues of the day.
- Pray for your pastor.
- Pray for your local church, and pray that the Spirit would infuse the missional imagination of God within your community.
- Pray that the Spirit would give your local church eyes to see your community in the same way God sees your community.

Day 1

BEGIN WITH THE WORD

Read 3 John 1-4

The third letter of John is personal in nature, much like his second letter. Like his first two letters, he writes to encourage continued faithfulness to the truth.

1. We are immediately introduced to Gaius. Describe below the ways John describes his faithfulness.

Early church tradition has been that Gaius is the same one mentioned in Acts 20:4 and was the first bishop of Pergamum in Asia Minor. We will never know for sure, but we do know that he is beloved. Gaius's faithfulness is praised by John, and one could imagine that Gaius's spirits were profoundly lifted after hearing these words. John not only rejoiced in Gaius's faithfulness but told him and others of his rejoicing.

As a pastor, it is often apparent that there are those in congregations who excel in the gift of encouragement, and there are others who, sadly, excel in the gift of discouragement. Sometimes, Christians do a better job criticizing those around them than lifting them up. But friends, this is not how it should be! When I made the difficult decision to resign from being a senior pastor, the church had the most beautiful worship gathering and celebration for me and my family. We were showered with gifts and cards. I will never forget sitting in my empty home on moving day opening every single letter. As I read encouragement after encouragement, story after story of how I or my family had blessed people, I wept and kept saying, "Why didn't I know they felt this way about me?"

Sometimes we wait too long to encourage others. Sometimes we think it but never share it.

2. Instead of journaling in your book today, pen a letter or write an email to someone who needs encouragement today.

Day 2

BEGIN WITH THE WORD
Read 3 John 5-8

Hospitality is a central theme in this passage. Gaius is remembered for his care and hospitality—likely for traveling preachers of the gospel. Today, we often think of hospitality as opening our homes and entertaining guests. But hospitality was so much more robust in John's context.

Hospitality extends far beyond the modern interpretation of simply hosting or entertaining guests. In these verses, hospitality is portrayed as an embodiment of love and sacrifice, echoing the ultimate act of love demonstrated by Jesus Christ. This form of hospitality is not merely about opening one's home but opening one's heart to others' needs, whether they be physical, emotional, or spiritual. It calls for a profound understanding of empathy and selflessness, urging believers to not love in word or speech alone but in action and truth. This passage fundamentally shifts the focus from a passive understanding of hospitality as a social obligation to an active, heartfelt commitment to serving others as a reflection of one's faith and love for God.

1. What have been instances where you have observed this kind of hospitality?

2. Read 1 John 3:16-18. What is the vision for hospitality described in these verses?

When we put this all together, we are reminded that truth isn't some sort of cognitive proposition or a set of intellectual beliefs; rather, truth is the committed participation in God's ways in this world—seen in our lives, actions, and thoughts.

As a mother of two young children, nothing makes my heart swell with joy quite like when they put into practice the ways of Jesus. When I watch them show compassion to other children, for example, this brings me more joy than when one brings home an A+ grade. (Now don't get me wrong, I love good grades!). God doesn't want us to merely become puffed-up Bible scholars; instead, he wants us to *live and walk* the truth.

3. What is one thing you can do to expand the practice of hospitality in your life?

4. Write a prayer below asking for the Spirit to propel you to a life of living, being, and walking God's truth.

Day 3

BEGIN WITH THE WORD

Read 3 John 9-10

We are now introduced to Diotrephes. Scholars believe that Diotrephes was present when the second letter of John was read to the church. They also believe that he was unhappy with John's warning and thus acted out. He chose not to submit to the wisdom of the pastor.

1.   Describe the ways Diotrephes walks outside of the truth.

2. Read Jesus' words from Matthew 20:20-28. The mother
    of Zebedee's sons is known to have been the mother of
    John, the author and elder of this letter.

    ■ What does she ask of Jesus?

    ■ What is Jesus' response?

3. How does this push up against Diotrephes's life?

It is possible that this teaching was at the forefront of John's mind as he wrote this letter.

Not only does Diotrephes like being first, but he is also described as hindering those who want to help other believers. Hindering the work of the kingdom is a problem addressed in other places in the New Testament.

4. Read each of the following passages and summarize who is being hindered:

■ Matthew 19:14

■ Mark 9:38-39

■ Luke 6:29

Obstructing the momentum of the kingdom was a serious issue in the early church and ought to be seen as one today. The antithesis to this is hospitality. Constantine Campbell writes in *1, 2, & 3 John* (The Story of God Bible Commentary):

> Hospitality in all its forms ought to flow from Christians as an acknowledgment of God's hospitality toward us. We were not "good guests," but he took us in and lavished us with love, mercy, and abundant provisions. He has even gone so far as to make us members of his family.

5. How might you aid in the momentum of the kingdom in your local church and community? Brainstorm ways you and your church can show hospitality to those on the front lines of ministry. What would it look like for you to partner with those who are proclaiming the truth?

Day 4

BEGIN WITH THE WORD

Read 3 John 11-15

Throughout our study, we've received a beautiful picture from John of the One we are to imitate—the One who embodies life, truth, love, hospitality, and light. John pastorally warns us to not imitate the evil one, the antichrist.

1. How can we discern if someone is representing God or the evil one?

Within this third letter, John has described three different men. It's no wonder, then, that John talks about imitation. He wants us to ask ourselves, Who will we imitate?

As a pastor, I often challenge our congregation to read the Bible as much as they are watching whatever news channel they are addicted to. It's funny—I can often tell when someone spends a lot of time watching one news source. Why? They imitate it.

We are surrounded by influencers beckoning us to imitate them. Much is at stake: our witness. When we imitate those who are not walking in the truth, we are also led away from the truth.

2. Who are you being influenced by more than Jesus and his Word? Have you ever thought about the things and people that are shaping you? Journal below about the outside influencers that are at risk of pulling you away from living God's truth.

3. Now take a few moments of silence. Ask the Spirit, What changes do I need to make in my life to be more formed into your likeness rather than that of worldly influencers? Journal below what you hear the Spirit saying.

CLOSING PRAYER

Jesus, I want to be like you. I want to know your truth and live your truth. I want others to see you in me and me in you. Give me eyes to see when I am being led astray and fill my heart with your love, so that I would be propelled toward hospitality and compassion and encouragement toward your people. Lord, may I be remembered for living a life that walks in your truth and your way. Amen.

Day 5

BEGIN WITH A CANDLE

Light your candle and place it in front of you. Find a comfortable place to sit.

Close your eyes and slowly breathe in and breathe out. As you sit, ask yourself, *What do I hear?* Listen to the sounds in the room and take note. Ask yourself, *What do I smell?* Take a deep breath and note the smells of the space around you. Ask yourself, *What do I feel?* Do you notice the floor beneath you or the chair your back is resting against? Take note of it. Now, ask yourself, *What do I see?* Draw your attention to the candle in front of you. Notice how it flickers and moves about and glows. Take mental note of the wonder of a flame. A simple spark fanned the flame into light.

Take a deep breath in, and as you do, thank God for his light. Exhale slowly and ask God to illuminate your mind in these next few moments. Repeat this until you are in the present and the Presence.

Open your Bible and read John 15:1-8 out loud. Now pause and be still before God. Thank God for his very good presence. Stay silent before God, listening for his voice. Listen for words that are echoing in your mind, perhaps from the Scripture.

Read John 15:1-8 out loud again. As you recite it, let it not just be words from a page, but let them now flow from your heart to God's heart.

Now pause again and be still before God. What words or phrases are impressed on your heart from the passage just prayed? Let's focus on them for a moment. Look in the passage for where that word or phrase might be written. Recite it again as a prayer to God. But let's reverse the pronouns as a prayer to God. Verse 1 would pray something like this:

"Jesus, you are the vine, and your Father is the gardener . . ."

Verse 5 would pray like this:

"Jesus, you are the vine, I am the branch . . ."

Repeat this exercise until you feel released from the moment. When you do, extinguish your candle and thank God for his presence.

BENEDICTION

This might be the close of the study, but it is far from the close of living the light of Christ.

May you go in the power of the Spirit,
proclaiming the light and truth of Christ.
May you walk in the light, live the light,
speak the light, and shine in such a way
that a weary world rejoices.
May you have the wisdom to discern
where there are idols or false teachers,
and may you repent when idolatry grips your heart.
May the light of Christ fill your heart in such a way
that you and your people become an island of mercy,
love, and grace in a world full of so much pain.
Amen.

ABOUT THE
AUTHOR

Tara Beth Leach (MDiv, Northern Seminary) is a pastor, author, and speaker. The senior pastor at Good Shepherd Church (Naperville, Illinois), she has also served communities in the Chicago suburbs as well as Southern California. As the author of *Emboldened*, *Radiant Church*, and *Forty Days on Being a Six*, the cofounder of Propel Ecclesia, and cohost of *The Pastor's Table* podcast, Tara Beth writes and speaks widely about women in ministry and church leadership. She has two beautiful and rambunctious sons and has been married to the love of her life, Jeff, since 2006.

A NEW BIBLE STUDY EXPERIENCE FROM INTERVARSITY PRESS

These Bible studies offer you a fresh opportunity to engage with Scripture. Each study includes:

- weekly sessions for a group of any size
- access to weekly teaching videos
- five days of individual study and reflection each week

The refreshing, accessible, and insightful content from trusted Bible teachers will encourage you in your faith!

With guidance from trusted Bible teachers, this new collection of Bible studies invites groups and individuals to take a closer look at Scripture and offers practices that create space for prayer and worship, lament, and wonder. Each six- to eight-week study explores Scripture through a thematic lens, beginning each week with a group session that includes both video teaching and discussion questions, followed by five days of individual study and reflection.

Like this book?

Scan the code to discover more content like this!

Get on IVP's
email list to
receive special
offers, exclusive
book news,
and thoughtful
content from
your favorite authors on
topics you care about.

 InterVarsity Press

IVPRESS.COM/BOOK-QR